BRIDGING THE GAP

ADDRESSING CHALLENGES AND OPPORTUNITIES IN INDIAN EDUCATION SYSTEM

SANDEEP MUKHERJEE

Made with ♥ on the Notion Press Platform
www.notionpress.com

DEDICATION

This book is dedicated to the resilient spirit and boundless potential of India's youth.

To the students who wake up early, study late, and pursue their dreams with determination and grit.

To the educators who inspire and guide, who encourage curiosity and foster a love of learning in their students.

To the parents who support and encourage their children, who sacrifice their time and resources to provide them with the best education possible.

To the policymakers and leaders who work tirelessly to improve the quality and accessibility of education for all.

May this book serve as a testament to the power of education to transform lives, empower individuals, and shape the future of our great nation.

Contents

Contents

Contents

Prayer

"Om Bhadram Karnebhih Shrunuyaama DevaahBhadram Pashyemaakshabhiryajatraah Sthirairangaistushtuvaamsastanoobhih Vyashema Devahitam YadaayuhSwasti Na Indro VridhashravaahSwasti Nah Pooshaa VishwavedaahSwasti Nastaarkshyo ArishtanemihSwasti No Brihaspatir DadhaatuOm Shantih, Shantih, Shantih"

OM. O Gods! Let us hear auspicious words from our ears. O reverent Gods! Let us behold propitious visions from our eyes, let our organs and body be stable, healthy, and strong. Let us do that which is pleasing to the gods in the life span allotted to us. May Indra, inscribed in the scriptures, bring us fortune! May Pushan, the knower of the world, grant us prosperity! May Trakshya, who vanquishes enemies, bestow us with blessings! May Brihaspati bring us success!

OM Peace, Peace, Peace.

About The Author

Sandeep Mukherjee is the name of a passionate teacher, a creative writer, an able administrator and above all a learner hungry for knowledge and experience. Coming from a humble background he started his career as a teacher and that is when he realized that he has a feel for students and learners. Holding two post graduate degrees followed by a degree in education and a post graduate diploma in counselling & family therapy, Sandeep has a vast experience of teaching students, training and guiding teachers and motivating school leaders through seminars and workshops.

His quest of education and knowledge made him travel extensively in India and abroad. In various capacities, from teacher to a school leader he has attended and presented his papers on a number of scholastic forums in England, the UAE, Singapore, Japan and Scotland to name a few. Many of his articles on education and contemporary issues have been published by national dailies, magazines of repute and web-portals viz., the Jagran Group, the Bhaskar Group, the Education World, the Education Today, the Pratiyogita Darpan, the Prabhat Khabar, the HT Media, the Career 360, the Knowledge Today – to name few of them.

Professionally equipped with adequate skills to coach teachers of the new age, Sandeep also has been certified as a quality auditor by the Quality Management International, UK and the National Accreditation Board for Education and Training, GOI. Sandeep is recognized well by his student-fraternity for his excellent skill of conducting quality circle time which he earned from professional training sessions by Ms Jenny Mosley's Quality Circle Time, UK.

The present book gives his vision about the changing facades of the education system of India straight from the days of Gurukul till the era of NEP 2020. By dint of his exposure and interactions with the best in education in various developed countries he very aptly paints the changing phases of education system of India vis-à-vis the top-ranking education systems of the world.

Being an ardent believer of the traditional values of Guru Shishya Parampara, Sandeep also maintains an extra edge when it comes to adopting and implementing technological interventions in the academic delivery systems of schools. After having served in various positions during his career in education, he is currently serving as Board Member of the largest education conglomerate of Uttar Pradesh, India, i.e., Sunbeam Group of Educational Institutions.

Preface

Education is one of the most powerful tools we have for building a better world. In India, education has always been held in high regard, seen as a means of social and economic mobility, and a pathway to a brighter future. However, as we enter a new era of rapid technological change, globalization, and environmental challenges, it is clear that our education system must adapt to meet the needs of a changing world.

The concept of "Bridging The Gap" represents a new paradigm in education, one that is focused on preparing students for the challenges of the future. It is not just about acquiring knowledge, but about developing the skills and mindset necessary to thrive in an ever-changing world. It is about cultivating critical thinking, creativity, collaboration, and communication skills, as well as promoting emotional intelligence, empathy, and adaptability.

This book, "Bridging The Gap: Addressing Challenges and Opportunities in Indian Education System," is a collection of essays, case studies, and expert opinions that explore the challenges and opportunities of education in the 21st century. It brings together leading educators, scholars, and policymakers to provide a comprehensive view of the education landscape in India, and to offer insights and strategies for improving educational outcomes and preparing our youth for a rapidly changing world.

The book is divided into four main sections. The first section provides an overview of the current state of education in India, highlighting key challenges and opportunities. The second section focuses on innovative teaching practices, exploring new approaches to teaching and learning that promote critical thinking, creativity, and collaboration. The third section delves into the use of technology in education, examining how digital tools and platforms can be leveraged to enhance learning outcomes. Finally, the fourth section discusses the role of policy in shaping the education landscape and presents strategies for improving education at the national, state, and local levels.

At its core, this book is a call to action. It is a call to educators, policymakers, and parents to work together to create an education system that prepares our youth for future challenges. It is a call to embrace innovation, creativity, and collaboration, and to build an education system that is inclusive, equitable, and responsive to the needs of all students.

I hope that this book will inspire readers to think deeply about the role of education in our society and to take action to create a brighter, more prosperous future for India's youth. I want to thank all of the contributors for their valuable insights and expertise, and I hope that this book will contribute to the ongoing dialogue about how we can create an education system that prepares our youth for a changing world.

SANDEEP MUKHERJEE - 15th March 2023

Prologue

Introducing India to the World: A Book of Humble Submissions

We are proud that India got entry in G20 and also its presidency to hosting G20 summit in India in 2023. We the citizens of India are eager to explore everything about India to the world and this is book is one of my humble submissions to that.

Disclaimer

The views expressed in this book "Bridging The Gap: Addressing Challenges and Opportunities in Indian Education System" are the sole responsibility of the author and do not reflect the opinions of any organization or individual. The author has written this book to celebrate the positive aspects of Indian education and to offer insights and strategies for improving educational outcomes in the 21st century. It is not intended to offend or harm any individual or group.

The author believes in the importance of open dialogue and critical thinking in education, as well as the fundamental right to freedom of speech and expression guaranteed by Article 19(1)(a) of the Constitution of India. This book is a testament to the author's commitment to promoting innovative and effective education practices, and to preparing India's youth for a rapidly changing world.

The author hopes that readers will approach this book with an open mind and a willingness to engage with the diverse perspectives presented. Through the power of ideas and collaboration, we can create an education system that is inclusive, equitable, and responsive to the needs of all students.

ONE

A Brief Overview of the Indian Education System

India is a land of diverse cultures, religions, and languages, and education has always been a critical part of its society. The Indian education system has undergone significant changes in recent years, from the traditional Gurukul system to modern-day classrooms. This chapter provides a brief overview of the Indian education system and its evolution.

The traditional Indian education system was based on the Gurukul system, where students would live with their teacher, learn about different subjects, and follow a strict routine. This system emphasized holistic learning, which included not just academic knowledge but also values, ethics, and social skills. Students would also learn from nature and the environment around them.

The modern Indian education system, on the other hand, is based on a structured curriculum that follows a standardized pattern. It is divided into primary, secondary, and tertiary education. Primary education begins at the age of 6 and goes up to the age of 14.

Secondary education lasts for two years and covers grades 9 and 10. Tertiary education includes higher education, vocational courses, and professional courses.

The Indian education system is governed by the Ministry of Education, which is responsible for setting the curriculum, guidelines, and standards for education in India. The National Council of Educational Research and Training (NCERT) is responsible for developing textbooks and syllabi for schools. The Central Board of Secondary Education (CBSE) and the Indian Certificate of Secondary Education (ICSE) are the two primary education boards in India.

The Indian education system faces several challenges, including high dropout rates, a shortage of skilled teachers, and a lack of access to education in rural areas. Additionally, there is a growing demand for higher education and vocational training, which has led to the establishment of more universities and technical institutions.

In recent years, the Indian education system has been undergoing a significant transformation, thanks to technological advancements and innovative teaching methods. The use of digital technology has helped bridge the gap between urban and rural education, and new teaching methods such as experiential learning and project-based learning are gaining popularity.

The Indian education system is also adapting to changing needs and expectations of the workforce, with an increased focus on practical skills and vocational training. The government has launched several initiatives to encourage entrepreneurship and skill development among youth.

Of Course, the Indian education system has come a long way from the traditional Gurukul system to modern-day classrooms. While there are challenges to overcome, the system is continually evolving, adapting to new technologies and methods, and preparing India's youth for a changing world. This book aims to provide readers with an in-depth understanding of the Indian education system and its current state, identify areas for improvement, and offer recommendations for a brighter future for Indian education.

(A) THE TRADITIONAL GURUKUL SYSTEM OF EDUCATION IN INDIA

The traditional Gurukul system of education in India dates back to ancient times when education was imparted in a holistic manner, encompassing not just academic knowledge but also values, ethics, and social skills. In this chapter, we will explore the Gurukul system of education and its relevance in modern times.

The term "Gurukul" means the place of the teacher or the teacher's home. Students would live with their teacher, known as a guru, and learn various subjects in a natural and immersive environment. The Gurukul system emphasized holistic learning, where students would learn not just from textbooks but also from nature and the environment around them.

The curriculum in Gurukuls was comprehensive, covering various subjects such as literature, philosophy, mathematics, economics, politics, astronomy, and medicine. Students would learn through oral instruction and observation, and the focus was on understanding concepts and applying them to real-world situations.

In the Gurukul system, education was not limited to a specific age group or gender. Students could start their education at any age, and education was open to both males and females. The system emphasized equality and provided education to students from all social backgrounds, irrespective of their caste or religion.

The Gurukul system was not just about education but also about character building. Students were expected to follow strict discipline and adhere to ethical and moral values. They would learn social skills and interact with people from various backgrounds, which helped in their overall development as individuals.

Despite its many advantages, the Gurukul system declined with the arrival of the British in India. The British introduced their education system, which was focused on creating a workforce for their colonial needs, and the Gurukul system was seen as outdated and primitive.

In modern times, there is a renewed interest in the Gurukul system of education, thanks to its focus on holistic learning and character building. Several Gurukuls have been established in India, which follow the traditional model of education. These Gurukuls have evolved with time, incorporating new technologies and teaching methods while maintaining the core values of the Gurukul system.

In conclusion, the traditional Gurukul system of education in India was a unique and effective model that provided holistic education to students. While the system declined with the arrival of the British, there is a growing interest in its relevance in modern times. The Gurukul system's emphasis on character building, social skills, and ethical values can serve as a valuable lesson for modern-day education systems.

(B) EVOLUTION OF THE INDIAN EDUCATION SYSTEM: KEY CHANGES AND DEVELOPMENTS

The Indian education system has undergone several changes and developments over time, from the ancient Gurukul system to the modern education system we see today. In this chapter, we will explore the key changes and developments that have taken place in the Indian education system and their impact on the education sector in India.

The Gurukul system, as mentioned earlier, was the earliest form of education in India, where students would live with their teachers and learn through observation and practical experience. The system was decentralized, with education being imparted in small clusters or ashrams, and there was no formal structure or curriculum.

With the arrival of the British in India, the education system underwent a significant transformation. The British introduced their education system, which was focused on creating a workforce for their colonial needs. The education system was centralized, with the establishment of universities and colleges that followed a set curriculum. The system was also highly elitist, with education being accessible only to a select few.

After India gained independence, there was a push for democratizing education and making it accessible to all. The government established various institutions such as the Indian Institutes of Technology (IITs) and the Indian Institutes of Management (IIMs) to provide quality education to students. The emphasis was on developing the technical and managerial skills of the youth, to aid in the country's development.

Over time, the Indian education system has evolved, with a focus on holistic education that incorporates values, ethics, and social skills. The government has introduced several policies and initiatives such as the Sarva Shiksha Abhiyan (SSA), the Rashtriya Madhyamik Shiksha Abhiyan (RMSA), and the Right to Education (RTE) Act, to make education accessible to all, especially those from marginalized communities.

The education system has also seen a significant shift towards digital education. With the proliferation of technology, there has been a rise in e-learning platforms, online courses, and digital classrooms. The COVID-19 pandemic has accelerated this shift, with the majority of education now being delivered online.

Despite these developments, the Indian education system still faces several challenges. There is a lack of quality education, especially in rural areas, and a significant gap in the quality of education between urban and rural areas. The education system also needs to focus on developing critical thinking skills and creativity, which are essential for success in the rapidly changing world.

Surely, the Indian education system has come a long way, from the ancient Gurukul system to the modern digital education system. The system has undergone several changes and developments, with a focus on democratizing education and providing holistic education to students. However, there are still several challenges that need to be addressed, and the education system needs to adapt to the changing world and equip students with the necessary skills to succeed in the future.

"India's education system has the power to transform lives and build a brighter future for all."

ϸϸϸ

TWO

Examining some Successful Education Systems of the World: Lessons for India

The Indian education system has undergone significant changes over the years, yet it still faces several challenges. The education system is often criticized for its focus on rote learning and lack of emphasis on critical thinking skills. In recent years, there has been a growing interest in examining the success of education systems in other countries and adopting their best practices. In this chapter, we will examine the success of education systems in countries such as Japan, Finland, and Vietnam, and the lessons that India can learn from them.

THE UNITED STATES OF AMERICA

Internationally celebrated teachers, glorified past history and inclusion of multiple cultures from around the world are what it appears to be when the world talks about the American Education System. There have been many Nobel Laureates, scientists, patent owners, Pulitzer awardees etc who have one or the other QS ranked Uni in the backdrop. Especially stress on STEM-based education, experiential learning, internships from a very young age and most importantly rubbing their shoulders with the world's select few best students who come to study in their country with the rich cultural background of their own country. This helps the Americans understand the concept of 'one world' and they learn the best practices of the best from across the globe.

Opportunities to earn while you work give the students the opportunity to understand differences in diversity. They also gain lots of experience in real-life situations as they get involved in work while they study.

Another noteworthy feature of the American Education System is promoting entrepreneurship. Unlike Indian students, whose aim is basically to get settled in life with a decent job, American students (even Indian students studying in America) start thinking about some or the other start-up as soon as they go out of college, some even drop out to control their volcanic enthusiasm to do something for the world.

THE UNITED KINGDOM

Revolutionary teaching styles and research-based pedagogies are something that comes from the Oxbridge culture in the country.

Students in the UK are expected to take interest in sports and other co-curricular in addition to their course of study. India's New Education Policy 2020 has a wide influence on the British Education System when we talk about the 5+3+3+4 levels of learning grids. The entire education machinery there is backed by a massive budget allocation every year. Even the elderly who could not get formal education or school dropouts after the mandatory stage of education is taken care of by the state-owned FE Colleges which teach them languages, science, mathematics, art and history compulsorily.

The most unique feature of the UK Education System is the 'tutorial structure' of classroom deliveries. The broad pedagogy remains the same, in this tutorial format of teaching, only a handful number of students are taken care of by one teacher-mentor of high caliber. This gives ample opportunity for learning and cross-learning in a niche setup of learners and teachers.

The evaluation system is yet another milestone in the UK which, by now, has spread across the globe almost as a pandemic, although, benefits students and teachers widely. The evaluation system is not based on 'marks scored' but rather is based on 'learning objectives met' and this is possible only by paying attention to individual students after identifying their core competencies and other interests.

JAPAN

The Japanese education system is widely regarded as one of the best in the world, with a strong emphasis on discipline, hard work, and dedication. The education system is centralized, with a set curriculum and uniform standards across the country. One of the unique aspects of the Japanese education system is the emphasis on moral and character education. Students are taught values such as respect, responsibility, and perseverance, which are essential for success in life.

Another noteworthy aspect of the Japanese education system is the focus on collaboration and teamwork. Students are encouraged to work in groups and learn from each other, which helps in developing social skills and a sense of community. The education system also places a significant emphasis on extracurricular activities such as sports and music, which helps in developing well-rounded individuals.

FINLAND

The Finnish education system is often cited as a model for education reform worldwide, with a focus on equity and quality education. The education system is decentralized, with each school given significant autonomy in designing its curriculum and teaching methods. The Finnish education system places a strong emphasis on creativity, critical thinking, and problem-solving skills. Students are encouraged to learn through practical experience, and teachers have a significant role in facilitating this learning.

One of the key factors contributing to the success of the Finnish education system is the high regard for teachers. Teaching is a highly respected profession in Finland, with stringent requirements for entry into the profession. Teachers are given significant autonomy in designing their lessons and are trusted to make decisions in the best interest of their students.

VIETNAM

Vietnam is another country that has made significant strides in improving its education system. The Vietnamese education system has undergone a series of reforms in recent years, with a focus on improving the quality of education and making it more equitable. The education system places a significant emphasis on science and technology, with a focus on developing the technical skills of students.

One of the unique aspects of the Vietnamese education system is the emphasis on teacher professional development. Teachers are provided with extensive training and support to improve their teaching methods and keep up with the latest developments in education. The education system also places a significant emphasis on extracurricular activities and community service, which helps in developing well-rounded individuals.

LESSONS FOR INDIA

The success of these education systems provides several valuable lessons for India. Firstly, there is a need to focus on values and character education, which are essential for the overall development of students. Secondly, there is a need to shift the focus from rote learning to critical thinking and practical experience. Finally, there is a need to place a significant emphasis on teachers' professional development and provide teachers with the necessary support and training to improve their teaching methods.

In conclusion, the success of education systems in countries such as USA, UK, Japan, Finland, and Vietnam provide valuable lessons for India. By adopting the best practices from these education systems, India can improve the quality of education and prepare its youth for a changing world.

"In India, education is not just a privilege, it is a fundamental right that must be accessible to all."

❦❦❦

THREE

The Rise of Innovative Teaching Methods in India: Examples and Case Studies

In recent years, there has been a growing interest in adopting innovative teaching methods in India, with a focus on improving the quality of education and preparing students for a changing world. Innovative teaching methods are characterized by a focus on active learning, problem-solving, and critical thinking. In this chapter, we will examine some examples of innovative teaching methods being used in India and the impact they have had on students.

CASE STUDY 1: PROJECT-BASED LEARNING

Project-based learning is an innovative teaching method that emphasizes hands-on learning and real-world problem-solving. The approach involves students working on a project that addresses a real-world problem, using skills and knowledge they have acquired in the classroom. One example of project-based learning being used in India is the Anandshala program, which is being implemented in government schools in the state of Rajasthan. The program involves students working on projects that address issues such as water conservation, hygiene, and waste management. The program has led to an improvement in student engagement and critical thinking skills.

CASE STUDY 2: FLIPPED CLASSROOM

The flipped classroom is an innovative teaching method that involves students watching recorded lectures or completing online assignments outside of class time, and then using class time for discussion, problem-solving, and group activities. One example of the flipped classroom being used in India is the Teach for India program, which is implemented in schools across the country. The program involves teachers creating videos that students can watch outside of class time, allowing for more interactive and engaging classroom activities. The program has led to an improvement in student engagement and critical thinking skills.

CASE STUDY 3: GAMIFICATION

Gamification is an innovative teaching method that involves incorporating elements of games into the learning process. The approach involves using game-like elements such as points, badges, and rewards to motivate students and make learning more engaging. One example of gamification being used in India is the

BYJU's learning app, which is one of the most popular education apps in the country. The app uses game-like elements to motivate students and make learning more engaging. The app has been successful in improving student engagement and academic performance.

CASE STUDY 4: COLLABORATIVE LEARNING

Collaborative learning is an innovative teaching method that involves students working together in groups to solve problems and learn from each other. The approach emphasizes collaboration, communication, and teamwork. One example of collaborative learning being used in India is the Enabling Leadership program, which is implemented in schools in Maharashtra. The program involves students working together in groups to solve real-world problems, and has led to an improvement in student engagement and critical thinking skills.

IMPACT OF INNOVATIVE TEACHING METHODS

The impact of innovative teaching methods on students has been positive, with a significant improvement in student engagement, critical thinking, and problem-solving skills. These innovative teaching methods have also been successful in improving the quality of education and preparing students for a changing world. Innovative teaching methods have also led to a shift in the traditional role of teachers, from being the primary source of information to being facilitators of learning.

Innovative teaching methods have the potential to revolutionize the education system in India, and prepare students for a changing world. By adopting innovative teaching methods such as project-based learning, flipped classroom, gamification, and collaborative learning, India can improve the quality of education and prepare its youth for a changing world. These innovative teaching methods have already had a positive impact on students, and there is a need for continued experimentation and adoption of innovative teaching methods in the Indian education system.

"The true value of Indian education lies in the power it has to uplift communities and create positive change."

ᑭᑭᑭ

FOUR

The Role of Technology in Indian Education: Post-pandemic Opportunities and Challenges

Technology has transformed every aspect of our lives, and the field of education is no exception. In India, there is a growing interest in incorporating technology into the education system, with a focus on improving the quality of education and preparing students for a changing world. In this chapter, we will examine the role of technology in Indian education, the opportunities it presents, and the challenges it poses.

OPPORTUNITIES

Technology presents several opportunities for the education system in India. Firstly, it can enhance the learning experience by providing access to a wealth of information and resources that were previously unavailable. The internet, for example, provides students with access to vast amounts of information on a wide range of topics, which they can use to supplement their learning.

Secondly, technology can make education more accessible and inclusive. With the rise of e-learning platforms and digital classrooms, students from all parts of the country can access quality education, regardless of their location. Technology can also provide opportunities for students with disabilities to participate in the learning process.

Thirdly, technology can help personalize the learning experience. With the use of adaptive learning software, students can receive tailored learning experiences that meet their individual needs and learning styles. This can improve student engagement and academic performance.

CHALLENGES

While technology presents several opportunities for the education system in India, it also poses several challenges. Firstly, there is a digital divide in the country, with many students lacking access to technology or the internet. This can create disparities in access to education and limit the effectiveness of technology in the classroom.

Secondly, the quality of technology in schools and universities is often subpar, with outdated hardware and software. This can limit the potential of technology to enhance the learning experience.

Thirdly, there is a risk that technology could replace the role of teachers in the classroom. While technology can be a valuable tool in the learning process, it cannot replace the value of face-to-face interaction between teachers and students.

Adopting and Implementing Technology in Education

- To fully harness the potential of technology in education, there is a need for a systematic approach to its adoption and implementation. This involves several key steps, including:
- Identifying the needs and priorities of students, teachers, and the education system as a whole.
- Ensuring that all students have access to technology and the internet, regardless of their location or socioeconomic status.
- Providing training and support for teachers to effectively use technology in the classroom.
- Ensuring that the quality of technology in schools and universities is up to date and meets the needs of students and teachers.
- Monitoring and evaluating the impact of technology on student outcomes, and making adjustments as necessary.

Technology presents both opportunities and challenges for the education system in India. While it has the potential to enhance the learning experience, improve access to education, and personalize learning, there are also risks of creating disparities in access, limiting the effectiveness of technology due to outdated hardware, and replacing the role of teachers. By adopting a systematic approach to the adoption and implementation of technology, the education system in India can fully harness the potential of technology and prepare students for a changing world.

"India's education system is a testament to the nation's commitment to empowering its people and building a better future."

FIVE

The Importance of Ethics and Values Education in India

The education system in India has traditionally placed a strong emphasis on academic achievement, with a focus on subjects such as mathematics, science, and language. However, there is a growing recognition of the importance of ethics and values education in preparing India's youth for a changing world. In this chapter, we will explore the significance of ethics and values education in India, its challenges and opportunities, and examples of successful implementation.

IMPORTANCE OF ETHICS AND VALUES EDUCATION

Ethics and values education refers to the teaching of principles that govern human behavior, such as honesty, integrity, responsibility, empathy, and respect. It is essential in developing a sense of social responsibility, civic engagement, and moral reasoning in students. In a rapidly changing world, where technology is transforming every aspect of our lives, ethics and values education becomes even more critical.

In India, where the culture is rich in spiritual and philosophical traditions, ethics and values education is essential to preserving the values that have sustained the country for centuries. It helps develop character and instills a sense of moral responsibility in students, preparing them for active citizenship and leadership roles in society.

CHALLENGES AND OPPORTUNITIES

The incorporation of ethics and values education into the Indian education system presents several challenges and opportunities. Firstly, there is a need for a systemic approach to the teaching of ethics and values, as it is not a subject that can be taught in isolation. It requires a comprehensive approach that includes curriculum design, teacher training, and assessment.

Secondly, there is a need for a shift in mindset, both in teachers and students, towards ethics and values education. This requires a shift away from the traditional emphasis on academic achievement towards a more holistic approach to education that recognizes the importance of character development.

Opportunities for ethics and values education in India include the rich cultural and philosophical traditions of the country. These can serve as a foundation for the teaching of ethics and values, providing students with a deep understanding of their cultural heritage and the values that underpin it.

SUCCESSFUL IMPLEMENTATION OF ETHICS AND VALUES EDUCATION

There are several successful examples of ethics and values

education implementation in India. One such example is the "Gandhi Ashram" program, which provides students with opportunities to learn about the life and teachings of Mahatma Gandhi, with a focus on his principles of nonviolence, truth, and social justice.

Another successful program is the "Value-Based Education" program, which is implemented in several schools across the country. The program focuses on the teaching of values such as honesty, integrity, and responsibility, and includes a range of activities such as role-playing, storytelling, and discussion.

Ethics and values education is an essential component of the education system in India, helping to develop character, moral reasoning, and social responsibility in students. While it presents several challenges, such as the need for a systemic approach and a shift in mindset, there are also several opportunities, including the rich cultural and philosophical traditions of the country. Successful implementation of ethics and values education can prepare India's youth for a changing world and help preserve the values that have sustained the country for centuries.

"Education is the foundation upon which we can build a more just and equitable society."

ᐅᐅᐅ

SIX

The State of Teacher Training and Professional Development in India

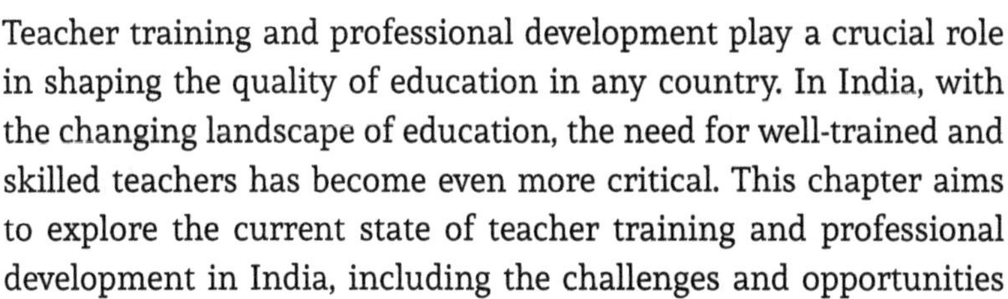

Teacher training and professional development play a crucial role in shaping the quality of education in any country. In India, with the changing landscape of education, the need for well-trained and skilled teachers has become even more critical. This chapter aims to explore the current state of teacher training and professional development in India, including the challenges and opportunities for improvement.

CURRENT STATE OF TEACHER TRAINING IN INDIA

The current state of teacher training in India is characterized by a lack of standardization and quality assurance. While the National Council for Teacher Education (NCTE) sets the guidelines for teacher education programs, there is a lack of consistency in the implementation of these guidelines across states and institutions. The training programs vary in duration, content, and quality, leading to an uneven quality of teachers across the country.

The government has taken several steps to improve teacher training in recent years, such as the introduction of the Integrated Teacher Education Programme (ITEP) and the Teacher Education Quality Index (TEQI) to assess the quality of teacher education programs. However, there is still a long way to go to ensure that every teacher in the country receives high-quality training.

CHALLENGES IN TEACHER TRAINING AND PROFESSIONAL DEVELOPMENT

One of the significant challenges in teacher training in India is the shortage of trained teachers. The teacher-pupil ratio in many schools is well below the prescribed norms, which means that teachers are overburdened and unable to provide quality education. The lack of motivation and low salaries are also deterrents for young people to choose teaching as a profession.

Another challenge is the inadequate focus on practical training and classroom experience. Most teacher training programs are theoretical and lack practical exposure, leaving teachers ill-prepared to handle the challenges of a real classroom. There is a need to introduce more hands-on training and internships to equip teachers with the necessary skills.

Professional development opportunities for teachers are also limited in India. In many cases, teachers do not have access to training programs or are not provided with the necessary resources and support to upgrade their skills. The lack of opportunities for professional development can lead to stagnation in teaching practices and a reluctance to adopt new methods.

OPPORTUNITIES FOR IMPROVEMENT

Despite the challenges, there are several opportunities for improving teacher training and professional development in India. One such opportunity is the use of technology to deliver training programs. Online courses and webinars can provide teachers with flexible and accessible learning opportunities, enabling them to upgrade their skills at their convenience.

Another opportunity is the involvement of private organizations and non-profits in teacher training. Several organizations are working towards improving the quality of education in India by providing training and support to teachers. Collaboration with such organizations can help bridge the gap in teacher training and professional development.

Teacher training and professional development are critical components of the education system in India. The current state of teacher training is inadequate, and there are several challenges that need to be addressed. However, there are also opportunities for improvement, and with the right focus and investment, India can create a robust and effective system of teacher training and professional development to prepare its youth for a changing world.

"In India, education is not just about academic excellence, it is about holistic development and personal growth."

❥❥❥

SEVEN

Navigating the Relationship Between Teachers and Students in Indian Schools

The relationship between teachers and students is an essential aspect of education. It has a significant impact on student's academic performance and their overall development. In Indian schools, this relationship is often characterized by a hierarchical and authoritarian approach, where the teacher is considered the ultimate authority figure. However, with the changing times and the adoption of new teaching methods, the relationship between teachers and students is also evolving. This chapter explores the changing nature of this relationship, the challenges that teachers face, and strategies to navigate this dynamic in a positive and productive way.

TRADITIONAL TEACHER-STUDENT RELATIONSHIP IN INDIA:

In traditional Indian schools, the teacher-student relationship is based on the guru-shishya Parampara, which is a hierarchical and authoritative approach. The teacher is considered the ultimate authority figure and is expected to impart knowledge to the students, who are expected to be passive receivers of that knowledge. The emphasis is on discipline, obedience, and rote learning. Students are expected to respect their teachers and follow their instructions without question.

CHALLENGES IN NAVIGATING THE RELATIONSHIP:

The traditional approach to teacher-student relationships presents several challenges for teachers. With the changing times, students are more vocal, independent and critical of authority figures. Teachers must navigate this changing dynamic while maintaining their authority and respect. Moreover, with the growing use of technology and digital media, teachers must also find ways to engage and connect with students on a more personal level.

STRATEGIES FOR NAVIGATING THE RELATIONSHIP:

To navigate the changing relationship between teachers and students, teachers can adopt several strategies. Firstly, teachers must adopt a student-centered approach that focuses on the student's needs, interests, and abilities. Secondly, teachers must build a positive and trusting relationship with their students by fostering open communication, mutual respect, and empathy. Thirdly, teachers must embrace new teaching methods, such as project-based learning, collaborative learning, and inquiry-based learning, that promote student engagement, critical thinking, and problem-solving skills.

In conclusion, the relationship between teachers and students is a crucial aspect of education. In India, the traditional approach to this relationship is characterized by hierarchical and authoritative structures, which present several challenges for teachers. However, with the changing times and the adoption of new teaching methods, the relationship between teachers and students is evolving. To navigate this dynamic, teachers must adopt a student-centered approach, build a positive and trusting relationship with their students, and embrace new teaching methods. By doing so, teachers can create a positive and productive learning environment that promotes student success and well-being.

"Education is the key to unlocking the limitless potential of India's youth."

❦❦❦

EIGHT

The Role of Parents in Supporting their Child's Education in India

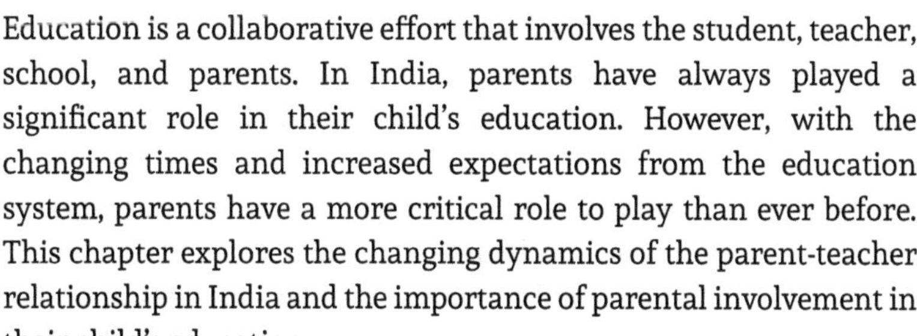

Education is a collaborative effort that involves the student, teacher, school, and parents. In India, parents have always played a significant role in their child's education. However, with the changing times and increased expectations from the education system, parents have a more critical role to play than ever before. This chapter explores the changing dynamics of the parent-teacher relationship in India and the importance of parental involvement in their child's education.

The traditional Indian education system places a lot of emphasis on parental involvement. Parents are expected to be actively involved in their child's education from a young age. They are encouraged to teach their children values, morals, and discipline. They are also expected to monitor their child's progress, attend parent-teacher meetings, and support the child in their studies. However, with the changing education system, parental involvement has taken on a more significant role.

Today, parents are expected to be more involved in their child's academic life. This involvement goes beyond ensuring their child attends school regularly, completes homework, and scores good grades. Parents are now expected to be a part of their child's education journey and help them navigate the various academic and career choices.

One significant change that has taken place in recent years is the increasing use of technology in education. With the rise of online learning and digital classrooms, parents have a more active role to play. They need to ensure their child has access to the necessary technology, monitor their online activities, and provide support when required.

In addition, parents also need to keep themselves informed about the changing education system and the different academic and career options available to their children. They need to be aware of the various entrance exams, eligibility criteria, and changing job market trends. This knowledge will help them guide their child in making informed decisions about their education and career.

Furthermore, parents need to encourage their children to develop critical thinking, problem-solving, and decision-making skills. They need to support their child in extracurricular activities and help them develop hobbies and interests. This will not only help the child develop a well-rounded personality but also enhance their academic and career prospects.

The role of parents in supporting their child's education cannot be overstated. A supportive home environment can make all the difference in a child's academic and career success. Parents need to provide emotional, moral, and financial support to their children and ensure that they have the necessary resources and guidance to achieve their goals.

In conclusion, parental involvement is an essential component of the education system in India. With the changing education landscape, parents have a more significant role to play in their child's academic journey. They need to keep themselves informed, provide support, and encourage their child to develop skills beyond academics. By doing so, they can help prepare their child for a changing world and ensure that they have a bright future ahead.

ÞÞÞ

"Indian education has the power to create leaders who can transform the world for the better."

❦❦❦

NINE

THE DEBATE OVER STANDARDIZED TESTING IN INDIAN SCHOOLS

INTRODUCTION:

Standardized testing has long been a contentious issue in education systems across the world. In India, this debate has been particularly intense, with many stakeholders questioning the efficacy and impact of standardized testing on student learning outcomes. This chapter aims to explore the debate over standardized testing in Indian schools, discussing the arguments on both sides of the issue, and examining potential solutions to the challenges posed by standardized testing.

THE PROS OF STANDARDIZED TESTING:

Supporters of standardized testing argue that it is an effective way to measure student progress and learning outcomes. They suggest that standardized tests help identify areas where students need additional support and enable schools to develop targeted interventions to improve student performance. Proponents of standardized testing also argue that these tests are objective and impartial, providing a fair and unbiased assessment of student abilities.

THE CONS OF STANDARDIZED TESTING:

Critics of standardized testing contend that these tests do not provide an accurate reflection of student learning and can be harmful to student development. They argue that standardized testing focuses too heavily on rote memorization and test-taking skills, rather than critical thinking and problem-solving abilities. Additionally, critics suggest that standardized tests can cause undue stress and anxiety for students, leading to a negative impact on their mental health.

ALTERNATIVE ASSESSMENT METHODS:

As the debate over standardized testing continues, educators and policymakers have begun to explore alternative assessment methods. One such method is performance-based assessment, which involves evaluating students' ability to apply their knowledge and skills in real-world situations. Another alternative approach is formative assessment, which involves continuous evaluation of student progress and provides ongoing feedback to improve student learning outcomes.

In conclusion, the debate over standardized testing in Indian schools is multifaceted and complex. While standardized tests may have some benefits, they also come with significant drawbacks. Moving forward, it is important for educators and policymakers to explore alternative assessment methods that better reflect the needs and abilities of students. Ultimately, the goal of any assessment method should be to promote student learning and development in a holistic and meaningful way.

"Indian education is not just about attaining degrees, it is about cultivating critical thinking, creativity, and innovation."

ÞÞÞ

TEN

EXPLORING DIFFERENT MODELS OF EDUCATION FUNDING IN INDIA

Education is an essential component of every society, and funding plays a crucial role in its development. In India, education funding has been a long-standing issue, with disparities in access to education and quality education being a significant concern. To address this issue, there have been several initiatives taken by the government and private sectors in exploring different models of education funding.

One of the most significant steps taken by the government of India is the introduction of the Right to Education Act in 2009, which mandated that every child between the ages of 6 and 14 years has the right to free and compulsory education. However, the implementation of this act has been challenging due to a lack of funding and resources. The government has tried to address this issue by allocating a significant amount of its budget to education funding.

Apart from government funding, private funding also plays a vital role in the education system of India. Private schools and universities have become increasingly popular in recent years, and many of them have made significant contributions to education funding. However, this has also led to concerns about access to education and the quality of education in private institutions.

Another model of education funding that has gained popularity in recent years is the corporate social responsibility (CSR) model. Under this model, companies are required to spend 2% of their net profits on social welfare activities, including education. Many companies have chosen to invest in education, and this has led to the establishment of several schools and universities.

Apart from these models, there are also initiatives taken by non-governmental organizations (NGOs) and individuals to support education funding in India. Many NGOs work towards providing education to underprivileged children, and several individuals have also set up foundations to support education.

While there have been several initiatives taken to improve education funding in India, there is still a long way to go. One of the major challenges is to ensure that the funds allocated are used efficiently and effectively to address the issue of access to education and quality education. There is also a need for more public-private partnerships to address this issue.

In conclusion, education funding is a critical component of the education system in India, and there have been several initiatives taken to address the issue of access to education and quality education. While there is still a long way to go, it is essential to explore different models of education funding to ensure that every child in India has access to quality education.

"In India, education is a tool for social and economic mobility, and a pathway to a brighter future."

ᑭᑭᑭ

ELEVEN

How Indian Schools are Preparing Students for the Future of Work

As the world evolves rapidly, so do the skills required to succeed in the workforce. With new technologies and industries emerging, Indian schools must adapt their curriculum to equip students with the skills and knowledge necessary to succeed in the future of work. In this chapter, we will examine how Indian schools are preparing students for the changing demands of the workforce and what more needs to be done to ensure that the next generation is adequately prepared for their future careers.

SKILLS FOR THE FUTURE OF WORK:

As the world of work becomes increasingly digital, students need to develop a wide range of skills that go beyond academic knowledge.

Indian schools are recognizing this need and are incorporating new approaches to learning that prioritize skills such as creativity, critical thinking, communication, collaboration, and problem-solving. These skills are essential for students to thrive in the rapidly changing work environment.

In addition to these core skills, students must also develop an understanding of emerging technologies such as artificial intelligence, machine learning, and robotics. Indian schools are increasingly adopting technology-based teaching methods to give students hands-on experience with these technologies, preparing them for the workplace of the future.

INDUSTRY-ACADEMIA COLLABORATION:

To ensure that Indian students are equipped with the skills and knowledge needed to succeed in the future of work, there needs to be greater collaboration between the education sector and industry. Indian schools are beginning to recognize the importance of this collaboration, and some are forming partnerships with businesses to offer apprenticeships, internships, and work placements to students.

These partnerships not only give students valuable work experience but also provide valuable insights into the skills and knowledge that will be required in the workforce. This information can then be used to develop relevant and effective curricula that meet the needs of the industry.

THE ROLE OF TEACHERS:

Teachers play a critical role in preparing students for the future of work. As the demands of the workforce change, teachers must adapt their teaching methods to equip students with the skills they need to succeed. Indian schools are increasingly investing in teacher training and professional development programs that focus on technology-based teaching methods, soft skill development, and industry-academia collaboration.

Teachers must also be equipped with the latest information about emerging technologies and industry trends to ensure that they are providing students with the most relevant and up-to-date information. The integration of technology in classrooms has made this easier, as teachers now have access to vast resources and information that they can use to supplement their lessons.

As the workforce continues to evolve, Indian schools must continue to adapt their curricula and teaching methods to ensure that students are adequately prepared for the future. The incorporation of technology, soft skill development, and industry-academia collaboration are all critical components of this preparation. By equipping students with the skills and knowledge they need to succeed, Indian schools can help ensure that the next generation is prepared for the challenges and opportunities that lie ahead.

"Education in India is a reflection of the nation's rich history, tradition, and intellectual prowess."

ppp

TWELVE

Addressing Issues of Inequality and Access in Indian Education

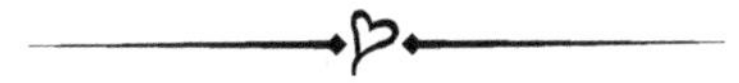

Education is a fundamental right that should be accessible to every individual, regardless of their socio-economic background or geographical location. Unfortunately, in India, access to quality education remains a challenge for many. According to the Annual Status of Education Report (ASER) 2020, only 16% of children in rural India have access to live online classes, compared to 33% in urban areas. Moreover, the report reveals a widening gap in learning outcomes between the privileged and the marginalized sections of society. Therefore, it is crucial to address issues of inequality and access to Indian education.

The Right to Education Act (RTE) 2009 was a landmark legislation that aimed to provide free and compulsory education to all children aged between 6 and 14 years. However, implementation challenges have hindered its success. For instance, many schools lack basic infrastructure such as toilets, electricity, and safe drinking water, which is a major deterrent for parents to send their children to school. Moreover, the quality of education in government schools has been subpar, which has led to a significant preference for private schools, leading to a growing divide in education quality.

To address issues of inequality and access, there are various strategies that can be implemented. Firstly, there needs to be an emphasis on improving the quality of education in government schools. This can be achieved by providing adequate infrastructure, increasing teacher training and professional development, and implementing innovative teaching methods that cater to the diverse needs of students. Additionally, the government should consider providing incentives to attract and retain qualified teachers in rural and remote areas.

Secondly, there needs to be a concerted effort to bridge the digital divide, especially in rural areas. This can be achieved by providing internet connectivity and devices to students, especially those from marginalized communities. The government can also explore innovative models such as community-based digital learning centers that can provide access to online education resources.

Thirdly, there should be an increased focus on inclusive education that caters to the diverse needs of students. This can be achieved by providing support services such as counseling, remedial classes, and inclusive classrooms that cater to students with disabilities.

Finally, there needs to be greater collaboration between the government, civil society organizations, and private stakeholders to address issues of inequality and access in education. This can be achieved by pooling resources and expertise to develop innovative solutions that cater to the unique needs of marginalized communities.

In conclusion, addressing issues of inequality and access in education is critical for India's development and progress. By prioritizing the quality of education in government schools, bridging the digital divide, promoting inclusive education, and fostering collaboration, India can ensure that every child has access to quality education, regardless of their socio-economic background or geographical location.

"The true value of Indian education lies in the way it instills values such as compassion, empathy, and kindness."

ᑭᑭᑭ

THIRTEEN

The Importance of Cultural and Linguistic Diversity in Indian Education

India is a land of diverse cultures and languages. Its education system is also known for its diversity in terms of the number of languages and cultural backgrounds. However, the challenge lies in creating an education system that can address this diversity and ensure that every child has equal access to quality education. In this chapter, we will explore the importance of cultural and linguistic diversity in Indian education and how it can be leveraged to create an inclusive education system.

CULTURAL DIVERSITY IN INDIAN EDUCATION:

India is home to various cultural groups, each with its unique customs, traditions, and beliefs. This diversity reflects in the education system as well. Many schools in India have introduced cultural activities as a part of the curriculum. Students are encouraged to learn about various cultures, festivals, and traditions. This not only helps in preserving diversity but also promotes harmony and understanding among students from different backgrounds.

Moreover, the curriculum has been modified to include the cultural context of different regions. For instance, history textbooks have chapters that cover the history of different regions, including local history. This has helped in making education more relevant and meaningful for students.

LINGUISTIC DIVERSITY IN INDIAN EDUCATION:

India is known for its linguistic diversity, with over 19,500 languages and dialects spoken across the country. In such a diverse linguistic landscape, it is imperative to have a multilingual education system. Recognizing this, the National Education Policy (NEP) 2020 has emphasized the importance of multilingualism and the need to promote mother tongue-based education.

Mother tongue-based education has several advantages. Studies have shown that students learn better and faster when they are taught in their mother tongue. It also helps in preserving and promote the diversity of languages and cultures. However, the implementation of mother tongue-based education faces several challenges, including a lack of trained teachers, inadequate resources, and resistance from parents and communities.

CREATING AN INCLUSIVE EDUCATION SYSTEM:

The cultural and linguistic diversity in India poses several challenges to the education system. However, it also presents an opportunity to create an inclusive education system that caters to the needs of every child. Inclusive education is an approach that seeks to address the diverse needs of learners by creating a learning environment that is supportive, equitable, and accessible to all.

Inclusive education requires a systemic change in the education system. It involves modifying the curriculum, training teachers, and providing adequate resources to ensure that every child has access to quality education. It also requires a change in the mindset of parents and communities to accept and appreciate the diversity of learners.

The cultural and linguistic diversity in India is a unique aspect of its education system. It reflects the richness and diversity of its culture and traditions. However, it also poses several challenges in creating an education system that caters to the needs of every child. To address these challenges, there is a need to create an inclusive education system that recognizes and celebrates diversity. This requires a systemic change in the education system, including the curriculum, teacher training, and resource allocation. With these changes, India can create an education system that prepares its youth for a changing world while preserving its cultural and linguistic diversity.

"Indian education is a journey of self-discovery, personal growth, and empowerment."

ᑭᑭᑭ

FOURTEEN

THE NEED FOR INTERDISCIPLINARY APPROACHES IN INDIAN EDUCATION

In today's ever-evolving world, the boundaries between disciplines are becoming increasingly blurred, and students need to be equipped with knowledge and skills that transcend traditional academic silos. Interdisciplinary education offers a solution to this challenge by integrating concepts and perspectives from multiple fields. In this chapter, we explore the importance of interdisciplinary approaches in Indian education and the benefits that students can derive from such an approach.

THE CHANGING NATURE OF EDUCATION:

Education in India has traditionally been organized along disciplinary lines, with students being exposed to a narrow range of subjects, each taught in isolation from one another. However, in the contemporary world, this approach is no longer sufficient. Advances in science and technology, for example, have transformed the way we think about health, the environment, and society. Disciplinary boundaries are becoming increasingly porous, and students must be prepared to navigate these complex and interconnected issues.

BENEFITS OF INTERDISCIPLINARY APPROACHES:

Interdisciplinary education offers a range of benefits for students. Firstly, it helps students to develop critical thinking skills by enabling them to identify connections and patterns across different disciplines. By integrating knowledge and perspectives from multiple fields, students can gain a more holistic understanding of complex issues, which can help them to solve problems more effectively.

Secondly, interdisciplinary education promotes creativity by encouraging students to explore new ideas and concepts outside of their disciplinary boundaries. This can help them to develop innovative solutions to real-world problems, which is increasingly important in today's rapidly changing global economy.

Thirdly, interdisciplinary education fosters collaboration by creating opportunities for students to work in teams with individuals from different backgrounds and areas of expertise. This can help them to develop communication and leadership skills, which are essential in today's interconnected world.

EXAMPLES OF INTERDISCIPLINARY APPROACHES:

In recent years, several educational institutions in India have started to incorporate interdisciplinary approaches into their curricula. For example, the Indian Institute of Technology (IIT) has launched a new interdisciplinary program that integrates courses in science, engineering, humanities, and social sciences. The program aims to prepare students to tackle real-world problems that require a multidisciplinary approach.

Similarly, the Indian School of Business (ISB) has introduced an interdisciplinary program that combines courses in management, economics, and social sciences. The program aims to produce graduates who are equipped to deal with complex business challenges that require a deep understanding of diverse disciplines.

Interdisciplinary education is critical to preparing students for the challenges of the 21st century. By breaking down disciplinary boundaries and fostering collaboration, creativity, and critical thinking, interdisciplinary approaches can help students to develop the knowledge, skills, and attitudes needed to tackle complex problems and create innovative solutions. The incorporation of interdisciplinary approaches in Indian education is a necessary step in preparing India's youth for a changing world.

"Education is not just about acquiring knowledge, it is about developing the skills and mindset necessary to succeed in life."

♡♡♡

FIFTEEN

Examining the Future of Indian Education: Predictions and Projections

The Indian education system has undergone significant changes in the past few decades. With the advent of technology and changing job market demands, the system has evolved to meet the needs of the modern world. However, there is still a long way to go in terms of achieving universal access to quality education for all.

Looking towards the future, there are several predictions and projections that can be made regarding the direction of Indian education. Some of the key trends and issues that are likely to shape the future of education in India are discussed below.

DIGITAL TRANSFORMATION:

One of the most significant changes that can be expected in the Indian education system is the widespread adoption of digital technology. With the growth of e-learning platforms, the use of artificial intelligence in education, and the development of digital textbooks, technology is set to revolutionize the way education is delivered and accessed in India.

PERSONALIZED LEARNING:

The rise of digital technology is also likely to lead to the adoption of personalized learning methods in India. By using data analytics and machine learning, educators will be able to tailor their teaching methods to suit the individual needs and learning styles of each student.

FOCUS ON VOCATIONAL TRAINING:

The changing job market demands in India are likely to result in a greater focus on vocational training in the education system. As the country moves towards becoming a knowledge-based economy, there will be a greater need for students to be equipped with practical skills that are relevant to the workforce.

INCREASED INVESTMENT IN EDUCATION:

The Indian government has recognized the importance of education for the country's development and is likely to increase its investment in the sector in the coming years. This is likely to result in greater access to education for all and the development of better infrastructure and facilities in schools and universities.

EMPHASIS ON MULTILINGUALISM:

With India being a diverse country with many regional languages, there is likely to be an increased emphasis on multilingualism in the education system. This will help to bridge the linguistic divide and enable students to communicate more effectively in a globalized world.

CONTINUED DEBATE ON STANDARDIZED TESTING:

The debate on standardized testing is likely to continue in the future, with some advocating for its continued use as a measure of student performance, while others argue that it does not accurately reflect a student's true abilities.

INCLUSION AND EQUITY:

The issue of inclusion and equity in education is likely to remain a key focus in the future. Efforts will need to be made to ensure that students from all backgrounds and socioeconomic statuses have access to quality education.

TEACHER TRAINING AND PROFESSIONAL DEVELOPMENT:

The need for better teacher training and professional development is likely to continue in the future. As technology and teaching methods evolve, teachers will need to be equipped with the necessary skills and knowledge to effectively deliver education to students.

Surely, the future of Indian education is likely to be shaped by the adoption of digital technology, a greater focus on vocational training, increased investment in education, and an emphasis on multilingualism. However, there will also be continued debates and challenges to be addressed, such as the issue of standardized testing and the need for greater inclusion and equity in education. By addressing these issues and trends, India can ensure that its education system is equipped to prepare its youth for a changing world.

"Indian education is a force for social change, bridging divides and empowering communities."

❧❧❧

SIXTEEN

The Role of Sports and Physical Education in Developing Holistic Learners

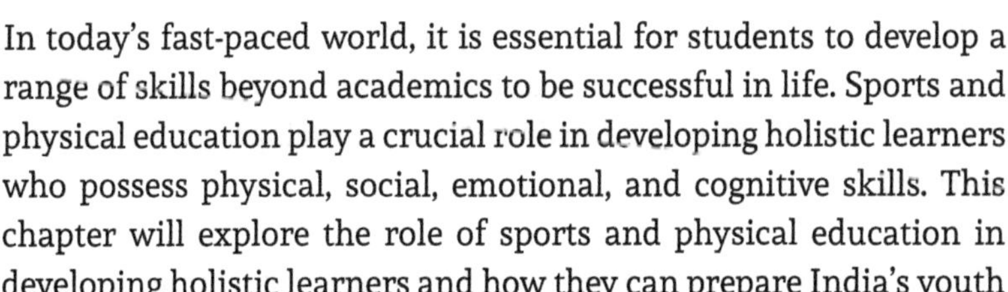

In today's fast-paced world, it is essential for students to develop a range of skills beyond academics to be successful in life. Sports and physical education play a crucial role in developing holistic learners who possess physical, social, emotional, and cognitive skills. This chapter will explore the role of sports and physical education in developing holistic learners and how they can prepare India's youth for a changing world.

THE IMPORTANCE OF SPORTS AND PHYSICAL EDUCATION

Sports and physical education offer a range of benefits for students, including the following:

Physical fitness: Sports and physical education promote physical fitness, which is essential for maintaining good health and preventing chronic diseases.

Cognitive development: Sports and physical education improve cognitive functions such as memory, concentration, and problem-solving skills.

Social skills: Sports and physical education help students develop social skills such as teamwork, leadership, communication, and collaboration.

Emotional well-being: Sports and physical education promote emotional well-being by reducing stress, anxiety, and depression.

Life skills: Sports and physical education teach students essential life skills such as time management, goal setting, and perseverance.

THE ROLE OF SPORTS AND PHYSICAL EDUCATION IN DEVELOPING HOLISTIC LEARNERS

Sports and physical education can play a critical role in developing holistic learners who possess physical, social, emotional, and cognitive skills. The following are some ways in which sports and physical education can contribute to the development of holistic learners:

Physical development: Sports and physical education promote physical development by providing opportunities for students to engage in physical activities that improve their strength, agility, coordination, and endurance.

Cognitive development: Sports and physical education promote cognitive development by enhancing memory, concentration, and problem-solving skills. Students learn to make quick decisions and adapt to changing situations, which are essential skills in a rapidly changing world.

Social development: Sports and physical education promote social development by teaching students' teamwork, leadership, communication, and collaboration skills. These skills are critical for success in the workplace and in building relationships.

Emotional development: Sports and physical education promote emotional development by reducing stress, anxiety, and depression. Students learn to manage their emotions, build resilience, and develop a positive self-image.

Life skills development: Sports and physical education teach students essential life skills such as time management, goal setting, and perseverance. These skills are essential for success in academics, career, and personal life.

HOW SPORTS AND PHYSICAL EDUCATION CAN PREPARE INDIA'S YOUTH FOR A CHANGING WORLD

Sports and physical education can prepare India's youth for a changing world by providing them with the following:

Adaptability: Sports and physical education teach students to adapt to changing situations and overcome challenges. This adaptability is critical in a rapidly changing world where students must learn to adjust to new technologies, work environments, and social norms.

Resilience: Sports and physical education teach students to build resilience and persevere through challenges. This resilience is essential in a world that is constantly changing and uncertain.

Collaboration: Sports and physical education teach students to work collaboratively towards a common goal. This skill is essential in a world that is becoming increasingly interconnected and globalized.

Innovation: Sports and physical education promote creativity and innovation by providing students with opportunities to explore new ideas and approaches.

Leadership: Sports and physical education teach students to develop leadership skills by providing opportunities to lead and mentor others. This skill is essential in a world where leaders must be able to inspire and motivate others towards a common goal.

Sports and physical education play a critical role in developing holistic learners who possess physical, social, emotional, and cognitive skills. These skills are essential for success in academics, career, and personal life. Sports and physical education promote physical fitness, cognitive development, social skills, emotional well-being, and life skills. By promoting physical fitness, sports and physical education help students to maintain a healthy body and reduce the risk of diseases such as obesity, diabetes, and cardiovascular disease. Additionally, engaging in sports and physical activity can enhance cognitive development by improving memory, attention, and concentration.

Moreover, participating in sports and physical education provides opportunities for social interaction and teamwork, which can improve communication skills, build confidence, and foster leadership abilities. It can also teach valuable life skills such as goal-setting, time management, and self-discipline.

Furthermore, sports and physical education can positively impact emotional well-being by reducing stress, anxiety, and depression, and promoting positive self-esteem and a sense of accomplishment. Through sports, students can learn to cope with adversity and failure, and develop resilience and determination.

Overall, sports and physical education are essential components of a well-rounded education that promote the development of physical, social, emotional, and cognitive skills necessary for success in all aspects of life.

"Education in India is an investment in the future, a commitment to building a better world for generations to come."

❦❦❦

SEVENTEEN

ADDRESSING MENTAL HEALTH AND WELLNESS IN INDIAN SCHOOLS

The mental health and well-being of students are important factors in ensuring that they receive a quality education. However, India's education system has often overlooked this aspect. According to a study conducted by the National Institute of Mental Health and Neurosciences, nearly 7% of India's population suffers from mental health problems. As a result, it has become increasingly necessary to address mental health and wellness in Indian schools.

MENTAL HEALTH ISSUES IN INDIAN SCHOOLS:

Indian schools have a long-standing tradition of academic rigor and discipline. However, this has led to an overemphasis on academic performance at the cost of mental health. The pressure to succeed has resulted in an increase in stress, anxiety, and depression among students. Additionally, issues such as bullying, discrimination, and social isolation have contributed to poor mental health.

THE NEED FOR MENTAL HEALTH AND WELLNESS PROGRAMS IN SCHOOLS:

To address mental health issues in Indian schools, it is important to implement mental health and wellness programs. These programs can provide students with the tools they need to manage their mental health and improve their overall well-being. By creating a safe and supportive environment, students can learn to manage stress, build resilience, and develop coping mechanisms.

INTEGRATING MENTAL HEALTH EDUCATION INTO THE CURRICULUM:

To ensure that students receive comprehensive mental health education, it is important to integrate it into the curriculum. This can be done by incorporating mental health topics into existing subjects such as biology, social studies, and physical education. Additionally, schools can introduce dedicated mental health classes that focus on developing positive mental health habits and behaviors.

PROMOTING MINDFULNESS AND MEDITATION:

Practicing mindfulness and meditation has been shown to reduce stress, improve concentration, and enhance overall well-being. Schools can introduce mindfulness and meditation practices to help students manage their mental health. These practices can be integrated into the school day, such as during morning assemblies or in between classes.

PROVIDING ACCESS TO MENTAL HEALTH PROFESSIONALS:

Schools can also provide access to mental health professionals such as counselors and therapists. These professionals can provide students with the support they need to manage their mental health. Additionally, they can work with teachers and staff to create a supportive environment that promotes positive mental health practices.

Addressing mental health and wellness in Indian schools is crucial in ensuring that students receive a quality education. By implementing mental health and wellness programs, integrating mental health education into the curriculum, promoting mindfulness and meditation, and providing access to mental health professionals, schools can create a safe and supportive environment that promotes positive mental health practices.

"Indian education is a beacon of hope, lighting the way for a brighter, more prosperous future for all."

ᑭᑭᑭ

EIGHTEEN

Empowering Students through Self-Defense Education: Strategies and Best Practices

In today's world, students face various challenges and risks such as bullying, harassment, assault, and violence, which can adversely impact their well-being and academic performance. Therefore, empowering students with self-defense education can help them develop essential life skills, boost their confidence, and prepare them for a changing world. This chapter will discuss the strategies and best practices for empowering students through self-defense education in India.

Self-Defense Education: What It Entails

Self-defense education is a set of skills and techniques that equip students with the ability to protect themselves in threatening situations. It involves teaching students how to avoid and defuse conflicts, recognize warning signs, and respond appropriately to violence or aggression. Self-defense education also emphasizes the importance of physical fitness, mental awareness, and emotional intelligence to enhance personal safety.

Strategies For Empowering Students Through Self-Defense Education.

The following are some strategies that can be adopted to empower students through self-defense education:

Integrating Self-Defense Education Into The Curriculum:

Self-defense education can be incorporated into the school curriculum as a part of physical education or health and wellness programs. This approach ensures that every student receives self-defense training and recognizes the importance of self-protection.

Conducting Workshops and Seminars::

Schools can organize workshops and seminars to educate students on self-defense techniques, strategies, and tactics. Such events can also provide an opportunity for students to learn from experts and practitioners in the field of self-defense.

Using Technology:

Technology can be used to enhance the effectiveness of self-defense education. For instance, virtual reality can simulate real-life scenarios, enabling students to practice and develop their skills in a safe and controlled environment.

Providing Ongoing Support:

It is crucial to provide ongoing support and reinforcement to students after they have received self-defense education. This support can take the form of mentoring, coaching, or follow-up training sessions to ensure that students retain their skills and remain motivated.

Best Practices For Self-Defense Education In Schools

The following are some best practices that schools can adopt to ensure effective self-defense education:

CCreating A Safe And Supportive Learning Environment:

Schools must create a safe and supportive learning environment that encourages open communication, mutual respect, and empathy. This environment fosters positive relationships among students and teachers, reducing the likelihood of conflict and violence.

Emphasizing Prevention:

Self-defense education must emphasize prevention strategies such as risk assessment, situational awareness, and conflict resolution. These strategies help students identify potential risks and avoid dangerous situations.

Empowering Students:

Self-defense education should empower students to take responsibility for their safety and well-being. This approach promotes self-reliance, self-confidence, and a sense of personal control, which are essential for personal growth and development.

Ensuring Gender Sensitivity:

Self-defense education must be gender-sensitive, recognizing the unique safety concerns and risks faced by girls and women. This approach ensures that all students receive training that is relevant and responsive to their needs.

Empowering students through self-defense education is a critical step in preparing them for a changing world. Self-defense education equips students with essential life skills, boosts their confidence, and promotes their safety and well-being. Strategies such as integrating self-defense education into the curriculum, conducting workshops and seminars, using technology, and providing ongoing support can be adopted to empower students. Best practices such as creating a safe and supportive learning environment, emphasizing prevention, empowering students, and ensuring gender sensitivity can also be adopted to ensure effective self-defense education in schools. By adopting these strategies and best practices, schools can create a safer and more supportive learning environment, enabling students to achieve their full potential.

"Indian education is a journey of self-discovery, where students are encouraged to explore their passions, interests, and potential."

ღღღ

NINETEEN

MEDITATION AND YOGA IN EDUCATION: BENEFITS, CHALLENGES, AND IMPLEMENTATION STRATEGIES

Meditation and yoga have been used for centuries as a way to improve physical, mental, and spiritual health. Today, meditation and yoga are becoming increasingly popular in schools and universities as a way to help students manage stress, increase focus, and improve academic performance. In this chapter, we will discuss the benefits of meditation and yoga in education, the challenges of implementing these practices in schools, and strategies for successful implementation.

BENEFITS OF MEDITATION AND YOGA IN EDUCATION

Meditation and yoga have been shown to have numerous benefits for students in educational settings. Here are some of the key benefits:

Stress Reduction: Meditation and yoga can help reduce stress levels, which can be particularly beneficial for students who may be dealing with academic pressure, personal issues, or other stressors.

Improved Focus: Both meditation and yoga can help improve focus and concentration, which can lead to improved academic performance.

Better Physical Health: Yoga can improve physical health by increasing flexibility, strength, and balance. It can also improve breathing and circulation.

Emotional Regulation: Meditation can help students regulate their emotions and develop greater self-awareness, which can be helpful for managing anxiety and depression.

Improved Relationships: Meditation and yoga can help students develop greater empathy and compassion, which can lead to improved relationships with peers and teachers.

CHALLENGES OF IMPLEMENTING MEDITATION AND YOGA IN SCHOOLS

While there are numerous benefits to implementing meditation and yoga in schools, there are also some challenges that must be addressed. Here are some of the key challenges:

Time Constraints: Schools may feel that they don't have enough time to add meditation and yoga practices to their already-packed schedules.

Lack of Training: Teachers and administrators may not have the necessary training to effectively implement meditation and yoga practices in the classroom.

Religious Concerns: Some parents and community members may have concerns that meditation and yoga practices are associated with specific religious beliefs.

Funding: Schools may not have the necessary funding to purchase yoga mats, and meditation cushions, or hire qualified instructors.

IMPLEMENTATION STRATEGIES

Despite the challenges, there are several strategies that schools can use to successfully implement meditation and yoga practices. Here are some examples:

Start Small: Schools can start by incorporating just a few minutes of meditation or yoga into the daily routine, gradually increasing the time as students become more comfortable with the practices.

Provide Training: Schools can provide teachers and administrators with training on meditation and yoga practices, or hire qualified instructors to lead classes.

Address Religious Concerns: Schools can address religious concerns by emphasizing the secular nature of meditation and yoga practices, and providing information about their benefits for mental and physical health.

Collaborate with Community: Schools can collaborate with local yoga studios or meditation centers to provide resources and support for implementing these practices.

Meditation and yoga have numerous benefits for students in educational settings, including stress reduction, improved focus, better physical health, emotional regulation, and improved relationships. While there are challenges to implementing these practices in schools, there are also strategies that can help schools overcome these challenges and successfully incorporate meditation and yoga into the curriculum. By doing so, schools can help prepare India's youth for a changing world by promoting mental and physical health, as well as developing important life skills such as self-awareness, empathy, and emotional regulation.

"In India, education is a powerful tool for breaking down barriers and promoting social cohesion and harmony."

ᚹᚹᚹ

TWENTY

CONCLUSIONS AND RECOMMENDATIONS FOR THE FUTURE OF INDIAN EDUCATION

This chapter aims to provide an overview of the key takeaways from the previous chapters and offer recommendations for the future of Indian education. The Indian education system is currently at a crossroads, with significant challenges and opportunities ahead. As the country gears up for the Fourth Industrial Revolution, it is essential to have an education system that is flexible, inclusive, and responsive to the changing needs of students and society.

KEY TAKEAWAYS:

Indian education has come a long way since the Gurukul system, but there is still a long way to go.

The current education system faces a range of challenges, including unequal access to education, outdated curricula, and inadequate teacher training.

There is a need for a more interdisciplinary approach to education that incorporates 21st-century skills such as critical thinking, creativity, and problem-solving.

Technology has the potential to transform education in India, but it must be used judiciously and in a way that does not exacerbate existing inequalities.

The importance of ethics and values in education cannot be overstated, and schools must prioritize this aspect of education alongside academic achievement.

Mental health and wellness must be given greater attention in Indian schools, and there is a need for greater awareness and resources to support students in this area.

RECOMMENDATIONS:

Redefine the goals of education:

The goal of education should be to prepare students for a rapidly changing world by imparting 21st-century skills such as critical thinking, problem-solving, creativity, and adaptability. The emphasis should be on developing students' capacity to learn, rather than just imparting information.

Focus on teacher training:

The quality of teaching is critical to the success of any education system. Therefore, the focus should be on providing high-quality teacher training and professional development opportunities that equip teachers with the skills and knowledge necessary to teach in the 21st century.

Promote interdisciplinary learning:

Indian education must move beyond traditional subject silos and adopt a more interdisciplinary approach. This will enable students to make connections between different subjects and develop a more holistic understanding of the world.

Embrace technology:

Technology has the potential to transform education in India by increasing access, personalizing learning, and improving student outcomes. However, it must be used judiciously, with a focus on addressing existing inequalities and ensuring that it does not replace human interaction.

Prioritize ethics and values education:

The importance of ethics and values in education cannot be overstated, and schools must prioritize this aspect of education alongside academic achievement. This will help students develop into responsible and ethical members of society.

Invest in mental health and wellness:

Mental health and wellness must be given greater attention in Indian schools, and there is a need for greater awareness and resources to support students in this area. Schools must provide students with access to mental health resources and support services to help them manage stress and build resilience.

The future of Indian education is full of promise, but it requires significant reform and investment. The education system must adapt to the changing needs of students and society and embrace new technologies and teaching methods. At the same time, it must prioritize ethics and values education, mental health and wellness, and a more interdisciplinary approach to learning. By taking these steps, India can prepare its youth for a changing world and create a more prosperous and equitable future for all.

"The true beauty of Indian education lies in its ability to inspire a love of learning and a lifelong pursuit of knowledge."

Citation And References

This book has been created by referencing various websites on the internet in order to gather valuable information and data. In addition to online sources, this book also draws upon the author's own research and includes references to relevant books in the library. By combining a variety of sources, this book provides a comprehensive and well-researched account of the subject matter. The author has taken care to ensure that all information presented is accurate and properly cited to give credit to the original sources.

Although every effort has been made to ensure the accuracy and completeness of the information presented in this book, human errors may still occur. If any reader discovers an error or omission in this book, I respectfully welcome their feedback and encourage them to bring it to my attention. Such feedback is valuable to me, and I will take all necessary steps to correct any errors and improve the content of this book in future editions. Thank you for your understanding and support.

Contact

Cell No: +91 9721452102

Address:
Flat No 406, Shanti Vimla Vihar Apartment,
Rohitnagar, Nariya, Sunderpur, Varanasi - 221005

E-mail: sandeepmmukherjee@gmail.com

|| LOKAHA SAMSTHAHA SUKHINO BHAVANTU ||

9 798890 260000

Printed by Libri Plureos GmbH in Hamburg, Germany